AMONISMS

Aphorisms by Amon Sherriff

Wisdom distilled through time and experience

Copyright © 2013 Amon Sherriff All rights reserved.

ACKNOWLEDGMENTS

I offer gratitude and thanksgiving to God and my heaven team, which includes my ancestors and my guardian angels. I am also thankful for my wife, Cina who is a clear voice of love amid the chatter and changes of life along with my adult children who have shown growth and good-heartedness beyond my dreams.

I am grateful for my mom, Yvonne Griffith, and for the bits of wisdom and personal experience she has so easily shared with me. Also, my dad, Preston Ross Sr., who taught me that the difference between people is what they do with the 24 hours given to them.

I am grateful for my extended family and friends that I have had the honor to make music with over the last 30 plus years, especially my brother, Bindu Gross, his family and their gift of love and creativity.

It has been my honor to have shared with so many hearts and ears who have been open to my words and insights throughout the years...and for them I am truly thankful!

TABLE OF CONTENTS

Love
Awareness
Gratitude
Encouragement

PREFACE
to the
Writings of Amon Sherriff

Approaching from a New Age Consciousness...we have to instill a wider and/or more complete spirit of acceptance and understanding of our power to affirm and confirm our reality. Reading these writings requires this awareness, along with a sense of being renewed through greater access to what can, and does, exist for our use and betterment.
"Insightfull" reading... Reading Insightfully...
Jimmi EsSpirit

DEDICATION

These writings are dedicated to the small voice within each of us that gives us answers and wisdom. I received these words when I needed them the most. The Messages on Love came during a time in my life when I was experiencing heartbreak and betrayal. The insights on encouragement were received in the midst of not feeling good enough. The instructions on gratitude and awareness came when life appeared dark and shadowy. It is my blessing to be able to share these Amonisms with you. May these words resonate with your heart and connect you to the light in your soul as they have for me through challenges and obstacles to emerge improved and better for the experiences.

SYMBOLS

The adinkra symbols below were originally created in West Africa. They represent concepts, values or aphorisms.

"By God's grace all will be well"
Symbol of hope, providence, and faith

"Wisdom Knot"
Symbol of wisdom, ingenuity, intelligence, and patience

"When you climb a good tree"
Symbol of support, cooperation, and encouragement

"The Heart"
Symbol of tolerance, and patience

"Gratitude"
A widely accepted symbol for gratitude and appreciation, representing the unfoldment and expansion of life.

LOVE, THE CONQUEROR

Love is the essence of our being. It is through the Love of God that we exist. Love is synonymous with God. I find it important to look at Love not only as a noun but also as a verb, adverb, pronoun and the subject, in other words, Love is what life is all about. Prayerfully these insights will expand your view of Love.

In all ways, Love
Love, weighs all

-Amon Sherriff

EXTEND LOVE TO ENCOMPASS THAT WHICH YOU DON'T UNDERSTAND

THE DIVINE REMEDY FOR HUMAN MISTAKES

WE ARE BLESSED

WITH THE ABILITY

TO **LOVE**...

NOURISH IT WITH

ATTENTION

CHERISH **THE**

HEALING PRESENCE

OF YOUR

LOVE!

SHARE THE TREASURES
OF YOUR HEART
GIVING LOVE
IS A HEALING ART

LOVE'S WEB WOVEN "WONDROUSLY" WITHIN, AROUND AND THROUGH OUR HEARTS CONNECTS US TO ALL THE GOODNESS WE CAN RECOGNIZE.

WE ARE HERE TO WORK

OFF

THE EDGES SO THAT WE CAN

FIT INTO THE

DIVINE CIRCLE OF LOVE.

LAY YOUR FOUNDATION IN FAITH AND BUILD UPON YOUR LOVE "CONSTRUCTION WORK"

LOVE YOUR WAY THROUGH THE HARD PLACES AND THE TOUGH SPACES, YOUR HEART IS STRONGER THAN YOU THINK.

THE ABUNDANCE OF LOVE WITHIN YOUR HEART WILL AMAZE YOU!

THE REALM OF TIME
IS TRANCENDED
WITHIN THE VIBRATORY
EXPERIENCE OF LOVE...
"THE INFINITE CONNECTION"

TURN A NO WIN
SITUATION INTO A
KNOW WHEN SITUATION.
KNOW WHEN TO GIVE...
LOVE IN ALL WAYS

THE FORM MAY CHANGE,
BUT THE PRINCIPLE
REMAINS THE SAME...
"LOVE IS FOREVER"

BE IMPORTANT TO YOURSELF...
YOU ARE THE ONE YOU HAVE
TO SHARE YOUR LOVE WITH.

AN ACT OF LOVE HAS A

SELF-CONTAINED

REWARD

START INSIDE AND WORK OUT,

ITS ABOUT FEELING GOOD

ABOUT YOURSELF

LOVE GROWS FROM WITHIN.

USE THE LEVERAGE OF
LOVE
TO CROSS THE BRIDGES
OF LIFE

LOVE IS THE BOTTOM LINE,
THE TOP AND BOTH SIDES...
REGARDLESS,
REGARD MORE... LOVE!

THE EVENTS OF LIFE ARE GIVEN ORDER BY GOD, LEARN
TO LOVE THE SEQUENCE.
"SUBMISSION":

WHERE LOVE FOR SELF ABIDES, THERE GOD ALSO RESIDES.

LOVE CALLS TO THE GREATER SENSE OF OURSELVES, URGING US FORWARD INTO THE CHOICES THAT LIE AHEAD...

THE INSPIRATION OF LOVE
DEVELOPS IN US THROUGH
THE WISE USE OF TIME.
SEE TIME AS A SERVANT NOT
THE RULER OF
REALITY.

FLEX ONE OF THE MOST
IMPORTANT MUSCLES IN
YOUR BODY... YOUR HEART

KNOW MORE LOVE!!

ALWAYS REMAIN OPEN TO LOVE, THE RULER OF ALL FEELINGS

WEAVE THE IN'S AND OUT'S OF LIFE INTO ONE GOLDEN THREAD OF *LOVE!*

WE CAN BE HELD IN CHECK BY OUR BELIEFS OR FREED BY THEM. BELIEVE IN THE POWER TO CHOOSE LOVE...
KNOW MORE LOVE!

REACH FOR MORE THAN YOU CAN GRASP, **LOVE** WILL BRIDGE THE GAPS.

LOVE IS THE CONNECTING FACTOR IN US, USE IT WISELY ON YOURSELF, THEN SHARE IT.

ROOTED FIRMLY IN LOVE WE YIELD TO NATURE'S DEMANDS AND CONTINUE TO GROW.

LOVE YOURSELF INTO IMPROVEMENT, A TRUE PATH OF ACCOMPLISHMENT

THE REALM OF TIME IS TRANSCENDED WITHIN THE VIBRATORY EXPERIENCE OF

LOVE...

"THE INFINITE CONNECTION"

AWARENESS

It is through greater self-awareness that our lives are opened to possibilities that didn't exist previously. Once the light of awareness has been turned on, darkness retreats, Continue to grow in the awareness of the great Love, beauty and spirit that is within each of us. These aphorisms are dedicated to becoming more aware of the power to co-create the reality that we experience..
GREATER AWARENESS,
GREATER LIFE!

WE ARE ALL IN THE SAME BIG ROOM, ROOM FOR SELF IMPROVEMENT.

THE WORLD IS FULL OF HURT PEOPLE, YOU CAN CHOSE TO NOT BE ONE OF THEM.

HEAL YOURSELF!

WHEN YOU MAKE GOOD USE OF YOUR TIME, NO ONE CAN WASTE IT...

RESPECT THE PRESENCE OF KNOWLEDGE, BOW TO THE GRACE OF WISDOM.

THE ETERNAL EXCHANGE OF SPIRIT AND MATTER ENABLES US TO EVOLVE THROUGH LIMITATIONS

OBSERVE YOUR THOUGHTS, THEN FOCUS ON THE ONES YOU WANT TO HAVE... THE DIVINE CHOICE OF FREE WILL.

WE ARE NOT ABLE TO JUMP TO THE FUTURE, WE HAVE TO GO THROUGH THE PRESENT... SEE THE PRESENT AS THE GIFT THAT IT IS.

TO MAINTAIN YOUR CALMNESS WHEN APPROACHED BY ANGER... IS A MASTER-PEACE OF LIVING!

LIFE IS A GREAT GIFT MADE WORTHY BY LIVING IT WELL.

MENTAL STABILITY IS MAINTAINED THROUGH "GRACEFULL" ACCEPTANCE OF CHANGE... "WHAT IS, IS!"

THERE IS MOTION IN STILLNESS AS THERE IS MUSIC IN SILENCE.

THE STORY WE TELL AND
THE WORDS WE SPEAK
ARE THE SPELLS WE
CAST...
BURDENS OR BLESSINGS?

SOME PEOPLE TEACH YOU
BY SHOWING YOU WHAT YOU
WON'T GO FOR!

AS YOUR HEART OPENS,
YOUR SPIRIT REJOICES
IN ACKNOWLEDGMENT...
ONENESS GROWS.

SINCERITY OF PURPOSE
HELPS YOU MAINTAIN
CLARITY OF ACTION.

AS WE ALLOW OURSELVES
TO THINK, SO SHALL WE
BECOME!

EVERY OPEN EYE IS NOT AWAKE!!

THE PRESENT MOMENTS ARE STEPS INTO YOUR FUTURE, ARE YOU STEPPING IN FAITH OR FEAR?

PRAYER; AN INVISIBLE FORCE WITH VISIBLE EFFECTS.
PRAYER WORKS!

MEDITATION SECURES WITHIN US THE TRUST OF TRUTH, TO MAKE KNOWN THE UNKNOWN

NOTHING TEACHES PATIENCE LIKE IMPATIENCE!

SUBMERGED IN THE TRUTH, THE HIDDEN TREASURE IS SEEN WITHIN AS THE RIVER OF LIFE FLOWS ON.

EMOTIONS CAN BE USED AS INSTRUMENTS OF LEARNING, DON'T LET THEM USE YOU.

THE HEART GROWS WITH ACCEPTANCE... AN ENLARGED HEART SOMETIMES BRINGS A PAINFUL PEACE.

YOUR LIFE IS A PRECIOUS PACKAGE PACKAGE HANDLE WITH PRAYER...!!

USE PEACE AS THE CONNECTION TO UNDERSTAND THE REFLECTION OF GOD'S GRACE IN US.

COINCIDENCE IS REDEFINED AS A "CO-SEQUENCE" OF LIKE VIBRATIONS

IN SEEING LACK, ONE'S LACK IS IN SEEING. SEE IT NOW... THE "FULLNESS" OF LIFE!

AS WE ATTEND TO HIGHER THOUGHTS WE RECEIVE BIGGER LESSONS FROM SMALLER THINGS

TAKE A MOMENT TO REFLECT ON AND RECEIVE MORE OF THE GRACE WITHIN THE MOMENT OF NOW...

BY MERGING STILLNESS INTO ACTION THE MIND IS CLEARED TO EXPRESS THE ESSENCE OF THE HEART.

SACRIFICE THE PAST AND "BE WHOLE" THE PRESENT MOMENT, THE FLAME WE CARRY NOW WILL LIGHT THE FUTURE.

CALMNESS AND CLARITY REIGN IN THE DOMAIN OF SPIRIT, GIVE YOURSELF OVER AND BE GUIDED.

IN THE SILENCE OF HUMILTY THE PRESENCE OF POWER IS ACCEPTED.

WHAT YOU LAY DOWN ALONG THE PATH OF LIFE, YOU WILL PICK UP...

GRATITUDE

When working from a perspective of thankfulness even mundane ordinary events take on new glow. When you are able to focus on gratitude you are able to see more to be "great-full" for.

"Count the blessings or the blessings don't count"
Anonymous

An "attitude of gratitude" will keep you at the right altitude.

BEING HAPPY COMES FROM

THE WELL ESTABLISHED

HABIT OF BEING

"THANK- FULL"...

DON'T FORGET TO

OUR WHOLE EXISTENCE IS A TUNE OF DIVINE HARMONY, AS WE PLAY THE SAME INSTRUMENT TOGETHER— LIFE

ALLOW THE JOY IN YOUR HEART TO PERSUADE YOUR MIND TO BE "THANK-FULL"

SORROW HAS BEEN KNOCKED OUT AND JOY HAS BEEN DECLARED WINNER AND STILL CHAMPION. NO SCHEDULED REMATCH!!

SPIRITUAL SELF-CONFIDENCE PLACES THE FOCUS ON THE POSITIVE.

JOY IS THE SENSE OF
GOD IN US.

ATTRACT THE BEAUTY IN
LIFE WITH THOUGHTS OF
"THANKFULLNESS".

PEACE...FOLLOWS A
"GREAT-FULL" HEART...

APPRECIATION BRINGS INCREASE...
SHARE TO UNDERSTAND THE TRUE VALUE OF HAVING.

LIFE AWAITS THE JOY IN YOU... FIND IT, FEEL IT, EXPRESS IT...!

BE STILL, BE WISE, BE..."THANK-FULL" !!

Encouragement

The dictionary definition of encouragement: is to inspire with courage, spirit or confidence, to promote, advance, help, and support. Encouragement can inspire us to draw on resources we may not have known we have. Look to find encouragement in small daily activities then share it with others. So often when we reach out to give we will also receive in ways that can be truly magical.

LET YOUR FAITH IN GOD BACK UP YOUR CONFIDENCE IN YOURSELF!

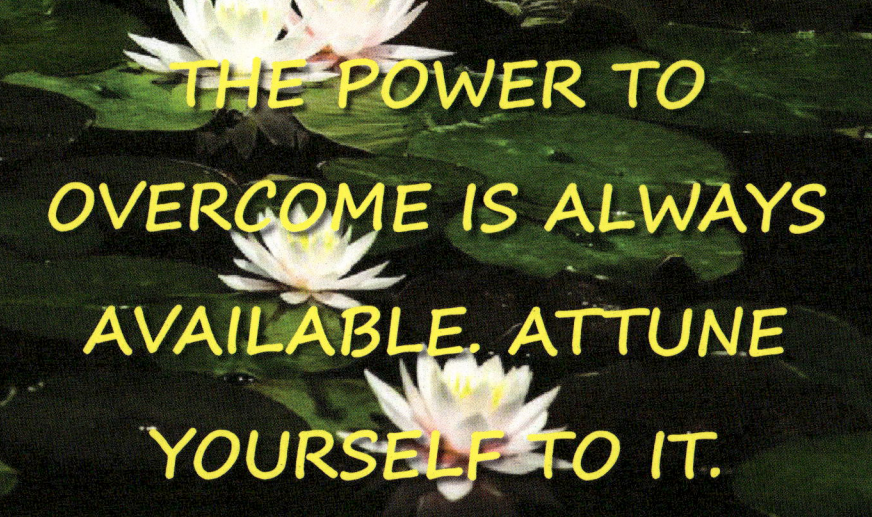

THE POWER TO OVERCOME IS ALWAYS AVAILABLE. ATTUNE YOURSELF TO IT.

FEEL THE EVER GROWING STRENGTH/CLARITY FROM WITHIN, MOVE WITH THAT POWER AND WITNESS THE RESULTS.

STAY ON THE PATH OF TRUTH THROUGH THE VALLEYS AND UNSURE FOOTINGS OF LIFE.

MOVE FEARLESSLY TOWARD YOUR DIVINE IMAGE WITHIN... FACE YOURSELF!

THE SWEET BREEZE OF CLARITY PREPARES US FOR THE STRONG WINDS OF CHANGE...

MAINTAIN THE INWARD DISCIPLINE TO ACHIEVE OUTWARD RESULTS. "DO WHAT YOU KNOW"

BY THE LAW OF DIVINE ORDER, GIVING HAS IT'S OWN REWARDS. CONTINUE...

BE CONFIDENT, BE CLEAR AND BE LOVED FROM WITHIN.

LIFE SPEAKS TO US OF TRUTH AND BEAUTY... LISTEN CLOSELY!

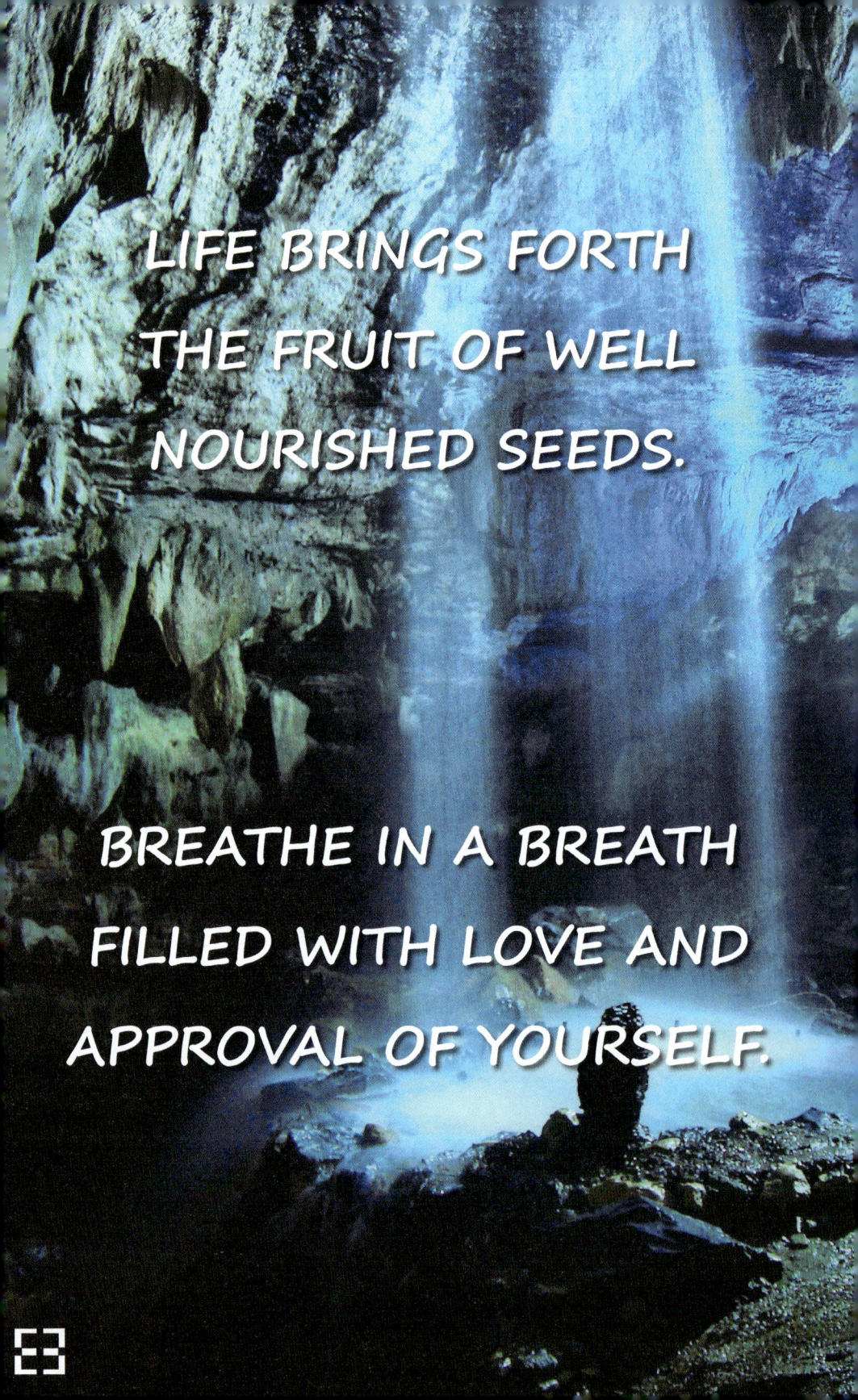

LIFE BRINGS FORTH
THE FRUIT OF WELL
NOURISHED SEEDS.

BREATHE IN A BREATH
FILLED WITH LOVE AND
APPROVAL OF YOURSELF.

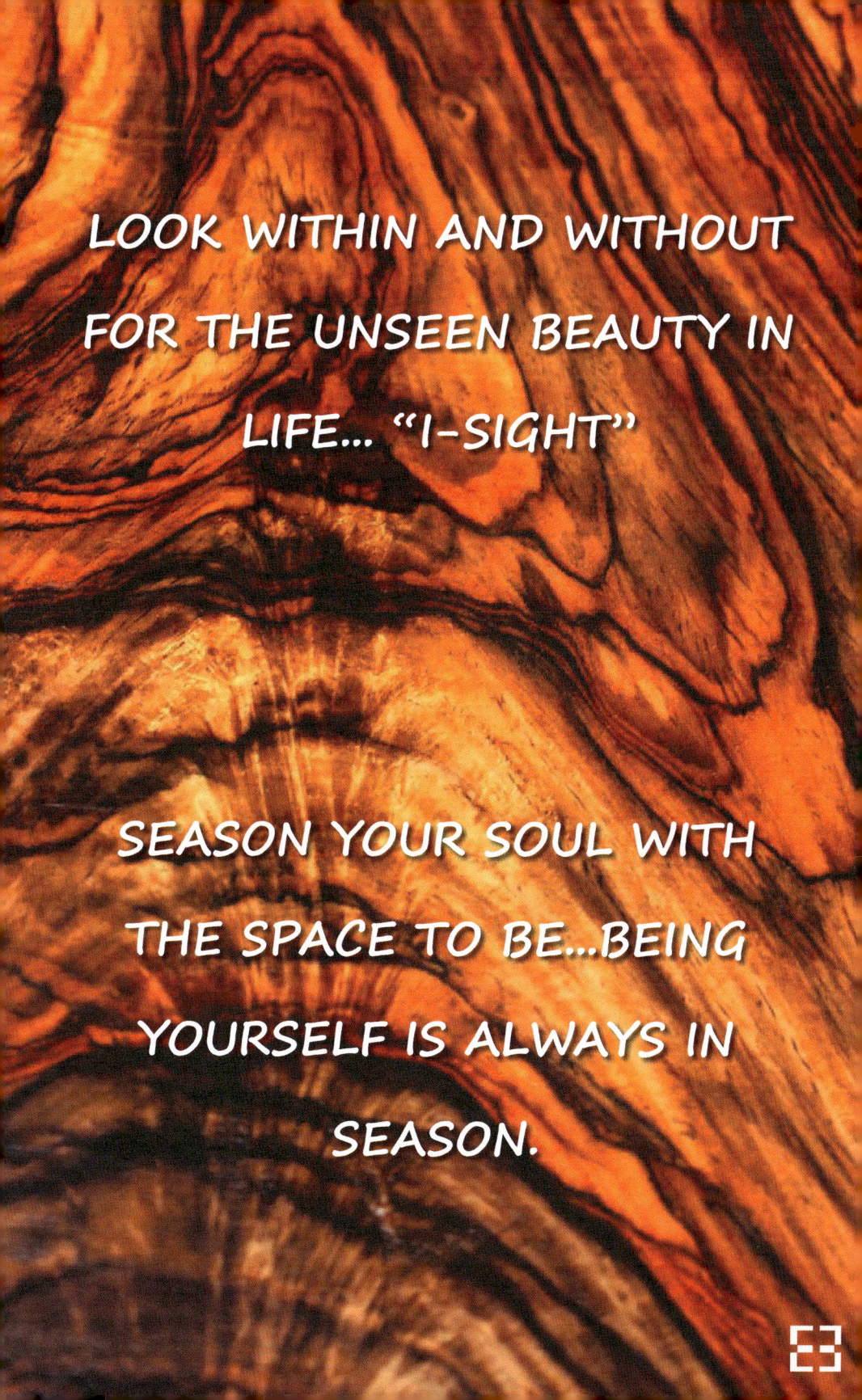

LOOK WITHIN AND WITHOUT FOR THE UNSEEN BEAUTY IN LIFE... "I-SIGHT"

SEASON YOUR SOUL WITH THE SPACE TO BE...BEING YOURSELF IS ALWAYS IN SEASON.

BE AS A BUDDING FLOWER, SUBMITTING TO THE WIND AND THE RAIN TO BLOSSOM IN THE WARMTH OF THE SUN.

PRESSURE CAN CREATE DIAMONDS, LET THE PRESSURE OF LIFE CREATE THE DIAMOND IN YOU.

WATCH AND SEE THE BEAUTIFUL SIGHT OF YOUR TRUST IN GOD WORKING FOR THE BETTERMENT OF ALL! DIVINE OBSERVANCE!

STAY "PRAYER-FILLED" AND KNOW YOUR PRAYERS ARE HEARD AND ANSWERED...

DON'T BE AFRAID OF GREATNESS. IT IS THE FATHER'S PLEASURE TO SEE YOU SUCCEED AND PROSPER.

MOVE WITH THE GUIDANCE OF YOUR HEART, IT IS LIGHTER NOW... NO NEED FOR THE HEAVINESS OF THE PAST.

TRUST THE PRESENCE OF GOD IN ALL SITUATIONS... A FAITH-FILLED VIEW.

MOVE FORWARD INTO THE FULLNESS OF LIFE WITH THE INNER LIGHT OF "SELF" SHOWING THE WAY.

LEARN TO CELEBRATE THE MOMENT OF NOW, CLAIM THE VALUE OF EACH MINUTE FROM WHICH REAL CHANGE CAN OCCUR.

BUILD YOUR SPIRITUAL MUSCLES BEFORE YOU NEED THEM

SET THE GOAL, HOLD THE VISION, DO THE WORK.

IN-COURAGE-MEANT FOR THE HEART!!

TIG TRUST IN GOD!

In Memory of Kenyatta Simon, Whose creativity and passion for what he Loved taught me to value my gifts and then to share them.

November 17, 1957 to January 7, 2014

Made in the USA
Columbia, SC
24 March 2018